by Michael Dahl   illustrated by Brian Jensen

Deep, Deeper, Deepest

Animals That Go to Great Depths

PICTURE WINDOW BOOKS
Minneapolis, Minnesota

Thanks to our advisers for their expertise, research, and advice:

Dr. James F. Hare, Associate Professor of Zoology
University of Manitoba
Winnipeg, Manitoba

Susan Kesselring, M.A., Literacy Educator
Rosemount-Apple Valley-Eagan (Minnesota) School District

Editorial Director: Carol Jones
Managing Editor: Catherine Neitge
Creative Director: Keith Griffin
Editor: Christianne Jones
Story Consultant: Terry Flaherty
Designer: Nathan Gassman
Production Artist: Angela Kilmer
Page Production: Picture Window Books
The illustrations in this book were created with pastels.

Picture Window Books
5115 Excelsior Boulevard, Suite 232
Minneapolis, MN 55416
877-845-8392
www.picturewindowbooks.com

Printed in the United States of America.

Library of Congress Cataloging-in-Publication Data
Dahl, Michael.
Deep, deeper, deepest : animals that go to great depths /
written by Michael Dahl ; illustrated by Brian Jensen.
p. cm. — (Animal extremes)
Includes bibliographical references (p.   ) and index.
ISBN 1-4048-1015-3 (hardcover)
1. Burrowing animals—Juvenile literature. 2. Deep-sea animals—
Juvenile literature. I. Jensen, Brian. II. Title.

QL756.15.D34 2005
590—dc22   2005003732

Animals live everywhere. They fly over the highest mountains and swim in the deepest oceans. They run over the hottest deserts and dive into the coldest waters.

Look down and see how low some animals can go. Watch as the numbers on the side of the page dip to extreme lows.

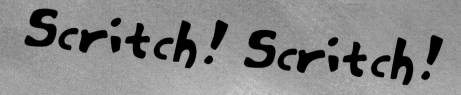

Scritch! Scritch!

An aardvark digs a deep burrow in the African desert. Its burrow is 40 feet below sea level.

Can any animal go deeper?

4

Sea Level

10 ft
(3 m)

20 ft
(6 m)

30 ft
(9 m)

40 ft
(12 m)

50 ft
(15 m)

60 ft
(18 m)

70 ft
(21 m)

80 ft
(24 m)

Yes! Green parakeets can! They go 1,000 feet below sea level. They swoop down to their nests inside a giant sinkhole in Mexico.

Can any animal go deeper?

Sea Level

200 ft
(61 m)

400 ft
(122 m)

600 ft
(183 m)

800 ft
(244 m)

1,000 ft
(305 m)

1,200 ft
(366 m)

1,400 ft
(427 m)

1,600 ft
(488 m)

Yes! The vampire squid can!
It glows 3,000 feet below sea level
in the Atlantic Ocean.

Can any animal go deeper?

Sea Level

500 ft
(153 m)

1,000 ft
(305 m)

1,500 ft
(458 m)

2,000 ft
(610 m)

2,500 ft
(763 m)

3,000 ft
(915 m)

3,500 ft
(1,068 m)

4,000 ft
(1,220 m)

Yes! The deep-sea angler fish can!
It goes 5,000 feet below sea level.
Its glowing lure attracts smaller
fish deep in the Pacific Ocean.

Can any animal go deeper?

Sea Level

1,000 ft
(305 m)

2,000 ft
(610 m)

3,000 ft
(915 m)

4,000 ft
(1,220 m)

5,000 ft
(1,525 m)

6,000 ft
(1,830 m)

7,000 ft
(2,135 m)

8,000 ft
(2,440 m)

Yes! A sperm whale can! It attacks a school of tasty squid 9,000 feet below sea level in the Indian Ocean.

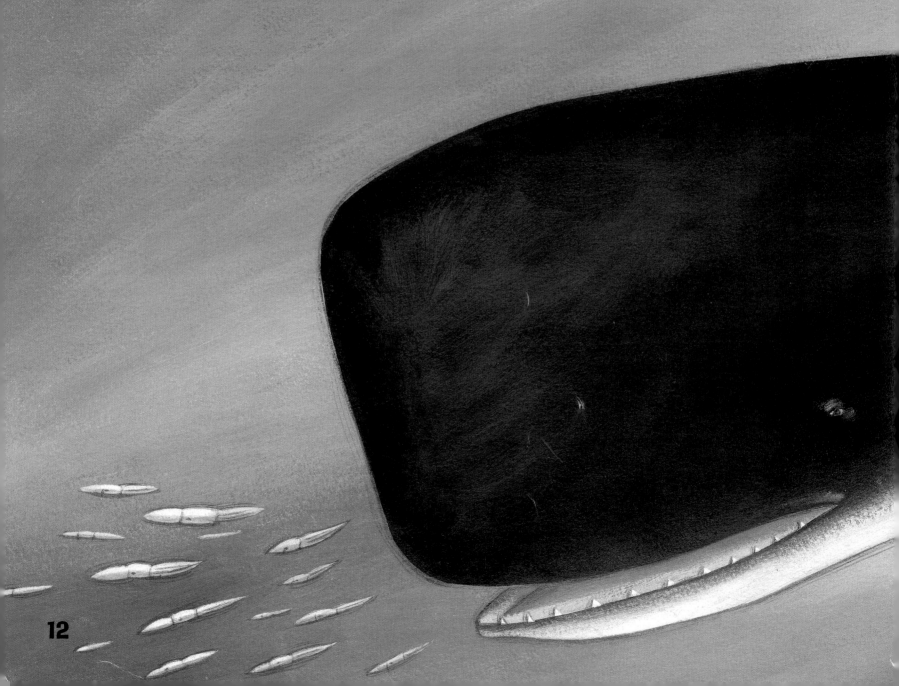

Sea Level

2,000 ft
(610 m)

4,000 ft
(1,220 m)

6,000 ft
(1,830 m)

8,000 ft
(2,440 m)

(9,000 ft.; 2,745 m)

10,000 ft
(3,050 m)

12,000 ft
(3,660 m)

14,000 ft
(4,270 m)

16,000 ft
(4,880 m)

Can any animal go deeper?

Yes! A fangtooth can!
It goes 10,000 feet below sea level.
It opens its big jaws and sucks in,
snatching up fish for lunch.

Can any animal go deeper?

Sea Level

2,000 ft
(610 m)

4,000 ft
(1,220 m)

6,000 ft
(1,830 m)

8,000 ft
(2,440 m)

10,000 ft
(3,050 m)

12,000 ft
(3,660 m)

14,000 ft
(4,270 m)

16,000 ft
(4,880 m)

Yes! A sea-star can! It snags floating plankton in its rough, branching arms 25,000 feet below sea level.

Can any animal go deeper?

Sea Level

5,000 ft
(1,525 m)

10,000 ft
(3,050 m)

15,000 ft
(4,575 m)

20,000 ft
(6,100 m)

25,000 ft
(7,625 m)

30,000 ft
(9,150 m)

35,000 ft
(10,675 m)

40,000 ft
(12,200 m)

Yes! A spiny sea cucumber can!
It creeps over the muddy seafloor
33,400 feet below sea level.

Can any animal go deeper?

Sea Level

5,000 ft
(1,525 m)

10,000 ft
(3,050 m)

15,000 ft
(4,575 m)

20,000 ft
(6,100 m)

25,000 ft
(7,625 m)

30,000 ft
(9,150 m)

(33,400 ft.;
10,187 m)

35,000 ft
(10,675 m)

40,000 ft
(12,200 m)

Perhaps.
Who knows what could go deeper?

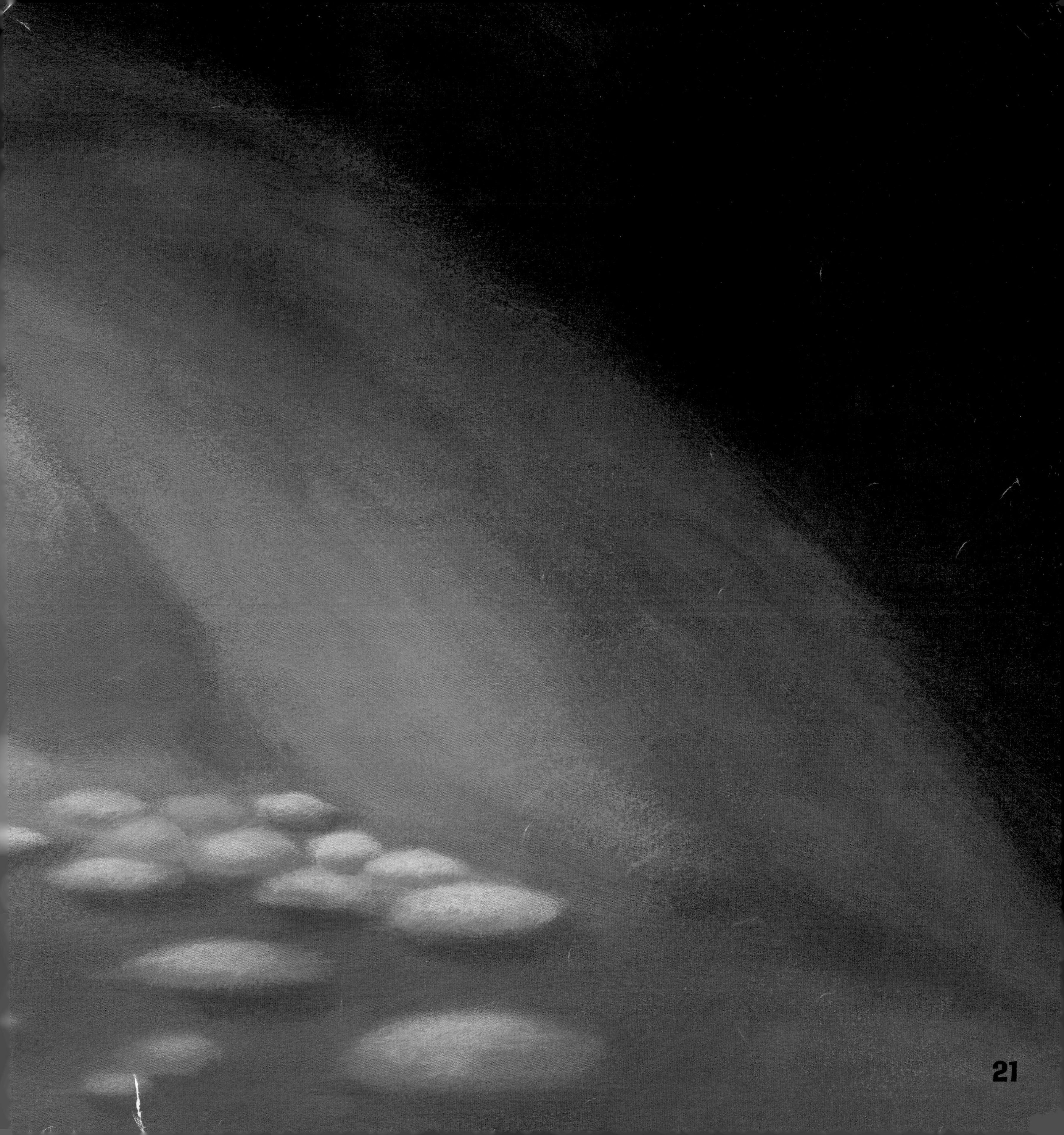

Extreme Fun

The word aardvark comes from a word that means "earth pig."

aardvark

In Mexico, green parakeets live in one of the world's deepest sinkholes. The sinkhole is so deep, people sky dive inside it!

green parakeet

Although small, vampire squid have the largest eyes for their body size of any animal.

vampire squid

With their very large mouths, deep-sea anglers can swallow prey larger than themselves.

deep-sea angler

The sperm whale is the deepest-diving mammal. It can dive to 9,000 feet (2,745 m) below sea level and stay under water for more than an hour.

sperm whale

Facts

Adult fangtooths have scary-looking fangs. Young fangtooths just have a single row of teeth.

There are 2,000 different types of sea-stars, or starfish, living in the oceans.

When a spiny sea cucumber is threatened, it squirts its internal organs at the predator. While the predator is distracted, the spiny sea cucumber escapes. It grows new organs quickly.

fangtooth

sea-star

spiny sea cucumber

Glossary

burrow—*a hole or tunnel in the ground made by an animal, usually for its home*

fangs—*long, sharp teeth*

lure—*bait used in fishing*

mammal—*warm-blooded animal that drinks milk from its mother*

plankton—*small plants and animals that float in water*

predator—*an animal that hunts and eats other animals*

school—*a group of underwater creatures that swim together*

sea level—*level of the surface of the sea used to measure heights and depths*

sinkhole—*a hollow hole in the ground; usually happens in limestone*

To Learn More

At the Library

Berger, Melvin. *Dive! A Book of Deep Sea Creatures.* New York: Scholastic, 2000.

Carson, Mary Kay. *In the Deep.* Philadelphia: Chelsea Clulbhouse, 2003.

Grupper, Jonathan. *Destination—Deep Sea.* Washington, D.C.: National Geographic Society, 2000.

On the Web

FactHound offers a safe, fun way to find Web sites related to this book. All of the sites on FactHound have been researched by our staff. www.facthound.com

1. Visit the FactHound home page.

2. Enter a search word related to this book, or type in this special code: 1404810153

3. Click on the FETCH IT button.

Your trusty FactHound will fetch the best sites for you!

Index

aardvark, 4-5, 22

deep-sea angler fish, 10-11, 22

fangtooth, 14-15, 22

green parakeet, 6-7, 22

plankton, 16-17

sea-star, 16-17, 22

sinkhole, 6, 22

sperm whale, 12-13, 22

spiny sea cucumber, 18-19, 22

vampire squid, 8-9, 22

Look for all of the books in the Animal Extremes series:

Cold, Colder, Coldest: *Animals That Adapt to Cold Weather*

Deep, Deeper, Deepest: *Animals That Go to Great Depths*

Fast, Faster, Fastest: *Animals That Move at Great Speeds*

High, Higher, Highest: *Animals That Go to Great Heights*

Hot, Hotter, Hottest: *Animals That Adapt to Great Heat*

Old, Older, Oldest: *Animals That Live Long Lives*